RESEARCH BRIEF JANUARY 2026

Connection, Trust, and Learning

Student Attendance in the Middle and High School Grades Following the COVID-19 Pandemic

Chronic Absenteeism Series 1

Elaine M. Allensworth, Meril Antony, William Delgado, and Marisa de la Torre

ACKNOWLEDGEMENTS

The authors would like to thank the many people who contributed to this study. The authors are very grateful to the staff at the Office of Student Support and Engagement, Chicago Public Schools and particularly the Attendance and Truancy team, for their continuous insight and support of this work throughout the development of the project, including Megan Hougard, Jake Brekelbaum, Zakieh Mohammed, Simone Moseley, and Amanda Smith. Thank you to our UChicago Consortium colleagues for providing input and feedback on the report, including Chen An, Jess Tansey, Bronwyn McDaniel, Jenny Nagaoka, David Stevens, and Alex Usher. We thank Consortium Steering Committee members Mariana Barragan Torres, Jessica Cañas, Lynn Cherkasky-Davis, and Brian Kelly for their thoughtful feedback. We also thank our colleague Shelby Mahaffie for conducting a thorough technical review of the brief, and Jessica Puller for copy editing. We are very grateful for support for this study from the Overdeck Family Foundation, Joyce Foundation, and Crown Family Philanthropies

We thank the Consortium Investor Council that funds critical work at the Consortium: putting the research to work, refreshing the data archive, seeding new studies, replicating previous studies, and making research equitable. Members include: Brinson Foundation, CME Group Foundation, Crown Family Philanthropies, Lewis-Sebring Family Foundation, Lloyd A. Fry Foundation, Joyce Foundation, Mayer & Morris Kaplan Family Foundation, McDougal Family Foundation, Robert R. McCormick Foundation, Polk Bros. Foundation, Spencer Foundation, Steans Family Foundation, Square One Foundation, The Chicago Public Education Fund, the Vivo Foundation, and two anonymous foundations. The Consortium also gratefully acknowledges the Lewis-Sebring Family Foundation, whose operating grant supports the work of the UChicago Consortium.

Cite as: Allensworth, E.M., Antony, M., Delgado, W., & de la Torre, M. (2026). *Connection, trust, and learning: Student attendance in the middle and high school grades following the COVID-19 pandemic.* Chicago, IL: University of Chicago Consortium on School Research.

This report was produced by the UChicago Consortium's publications and communications staff: Bronwyn McDaniel, Communications Manager, and Jessica Puller, Senior Communications Strategist.

Graphic Design: Jeff Hall Design
Photography: iStock
Editing: Bronwyn McDaniel and Jessica Puller

01.2026/PDF/jh.design@rcn.com

Introduction

In Chicago and districts across the world, school absenteeism increased dramatically following the COVID-19 pandemic, posing challenges for practitioners and raising questions about implications for student outcomes. Nationally, rates of chronic absenteeism (defined as missing 10% or more of school days, which is about 18 days in Chicago[1]) jumped to over 28% of students in 2022, compared to about 15% of students in years (2019) just prior to the pandemic.[2] Not only were more students chronically absent, but more students were very chronically absent—missing 20% or more days of school (which is 36 days or more). And there were fewer students with strong attendance (missing 5% or less, which is about nine days of school a year).[3] In the Chicago Public Schools (CPS) the percentage of students who were chronically absent nearly doubled from 24% in 2019 to 45% in 2022.[4]

Research prior to the COVID-19 pandemic consistently demonstrated strong links between school attendance and students' grades and test scores.[5] But with changing conditions in recent years—where absences are more common, many adults work from home, new policies around grades and attendance have been enacted,[6] and there is a greater use of technology in communication and education (e.g., online access to assignments and course materials)—we have repeatedly heard questions about whether the pre-pandemic connections between attendance, grades, and test scores hold for today's students in today's schools.

We have also heard questions about whether there is much that schools can do to address high rates of absence. School absences are strongly affected by the resources families can bring to bear to get students to school on time and ready to learn, meeting needs for transportation, food, clothing, stable housing, physical and mental health, and care for other family members.[7] Given all these potential drivers, there are questions about whether strategies that focus on schools would be likely to have much of an impact.

There are also many questions about the potential influence of different school and neighborhood factors on school absences. One of those factors is school climate. The degree to which a school's climate is welcoming, with positive relationships, is frequently mentioned as a contributing factor to attendance.[8] But how much do these factors matter now that absence rates are so high and conditions in the broader society have changed?

This brief summarizes findings from the first year of a multi-year study examining the causes, consequences, and impacts of absenteeism in Chicago in post-pandemic years relative to pre-pandemic years among students in grades 6-11. We focus on the middle and high school grades because these are years when many students show a rise in absences, relative to their attendance in the elementary grades.

---

1 Illinois law requires a minimum of 176 days of actual pupil attendance. To ensure this, the school year calendar must include a minimum of 185 total days to account for the 176 student attendance days, five emergency days, professional development, and any other days off.

2 Malkus (2025).

3 Barshay (2025, August 4).

4 Schmid (2023, January 30).

5 Allensworth & Easton 2007; Allensworth et al. (2014); Allensworth et al. (2025); Aucejo & Romano (2016); Gottfried (2014); Ready (2010); Kirksey (2019).

6 For example, starting in 2022, Illinois allowed students to take up to five excused mental health days per year. During the pandemic, some schools changed their policies to be more flexible about turning in work late and eliminating grades of zero.

7 Aucejo & Romano (2016); Forrest, Bevans, Riley, Crespo, & Louis (2011); Garcia & Weiss (2018); Attendance Works & Healthy Schools Campaign (2015).

8 Attendance Works (2025).

Research Questions

This brief addresses four research questions about students in grades 6-11:

RQ1: How have students' absence rates changed in post-pandemic years, compared to pre-pandemic years?

RQ2: Do absences still matter for student achievement as much as they did before the pandemic?

RQ3: To what extent are there systematic differences in students' absence rates by school?

- How large are school differences after taking into account differences in their students' neighborhoods, demographic backgrounds, test scores, and attendance in prior years?

RQ4: What is the influence of school climate on absenteeism, and has its influence changed since the pandemic?

- Which aspects of school climate are most influential in supporting students' attendance?

Data & Methods

This study uses administrative records from schools serving students in grades 6-11 in CPS, linking student attendance and achievement to school- and neighborhood-level data sources, including *5Essentials* school climate surveys and census-based community data, such as poverty and unemployment.[9] Analyses compare absenteeism and achievement before and after the pandemic's onset: in pre-pandemic years (2016–17, 2017–18, 2018–19), relative to post-pandemic years (2021–22, 2022–23, and 2023–24), using data on the population of students in CPS in those years who were enrolled for at least 20 days in the year. This differs slightly from the district criteria for calculating attendance rates which is based on students enrolled for at least 11 days. Charter schools are included in all analyses except those related student attendance to their grades (GPAs) as their transcript data are not collected centrally.

For the third research question, we begin with descriptive displays of data and then show the results of cross-nested hierarchical linear models (HLMs) that isolate the separate influences of schools and neighborhoods. We then employ rigorous controls to isolate school effects net of differences in the students they serve, controlling for students' background characteristics and the average prior attendance and test scores in grades 3-5 when studying absences in grades 6-8, or in grades 6-8 when studying grades 9-11. These models control out any effects the school might have had on absences in years prior (e.g., grades 3-5) when looking at school differences in grades 6-8, which likely results in under-identifying school effects in the middle grades. However, it ensures that we are not attributing to schools' differences that result because of serving different students.

For the fourth research question, we introduce measures of school climate into the cross-nested HLMs described above that include rigorous controls for student background and prior achievement and attendance. School climate measures come from school average responses on annual surveys of students and teachers in CPS, which have response rates ranging from 71% to 82% among students and 72% to 81% among teachers from 2017 to 2024 (excluding pandemic years). To provide a sense of the strength of the relationships, we use the coefficients from the model to estimate the difference in absence rates for students at schools that are at about the 25th and 75th percentiles in terms of school climate, controlling other factors in the model.

These are initial findings from this study; further stages of the work will examine specific school and neighborhood factors and investigate causal relationships. Details of the current analyses can be found in the Supplementary Technical Appendix.

9 Data on grade 12 were not included in the study because the days missed for twelfth-graders include days not in school after graduation, which takes place before the school year is over. This inflates the rates and makes them inaccurate for twelfth graders.

Key Finding 01

Research Question 1

Chronic absenteeism increased by about 20 percentage points in the post-pandemic years: Fewer students had low absence rates and more had extremely high absence rates

Following the pandemic, there was a dramatic surge in chronic absenteeism at all grade levels. Students are considered chronically absent when they miss 10% or more of school days. **Figure 1** shows the percentage of students who were chronically absent in grades 6-11 three years before the pandemic and three years after the pandemic. Before the pandemic (2017-2019), chronic absenteeism rates in the middle grades were at or just over 10%, and that number jumped to 33% in 2022 after schools returned to full in-person instruction that year. Similar increases were present for high school grades; between 27% to 37% of students were chronically absent before the pandemic (2017), and that increased to 49% to 57% in 2022. The rates of chronic absenteeism remained high through the 2023–24 school year, showing a persistent shift in attendance patterns.

FIGURE 1

The percent of students who were chronically absent increased by 20 percentage points after the pandemic

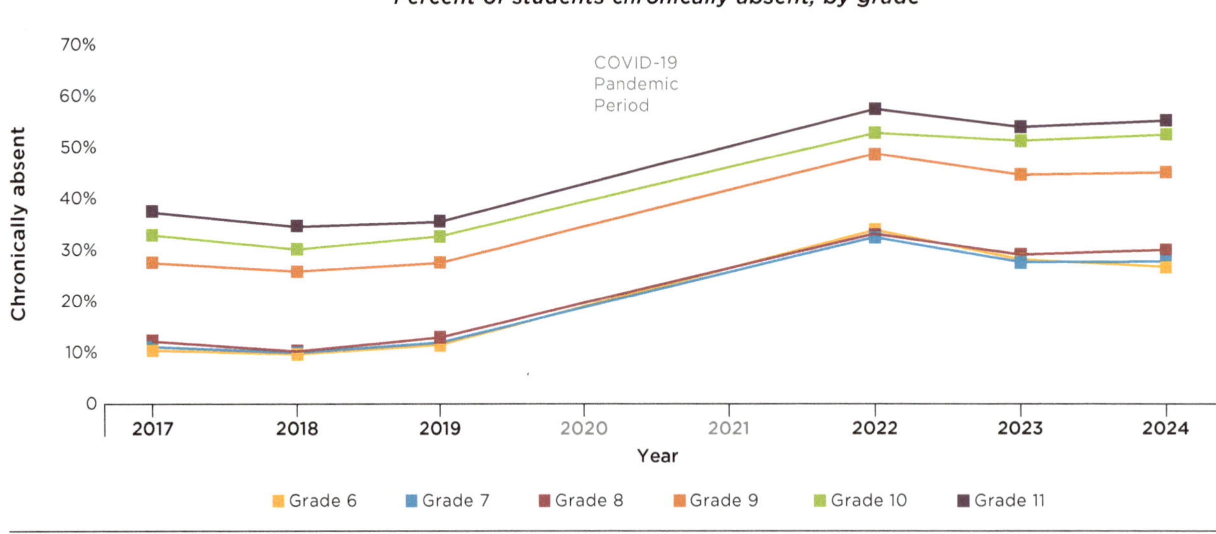

Note: Chronic absenteeism is defined as missing 10% or more of enrolled school days.

Dividing absence rates into more detailed categories reveals not only that more students were chronically absent, but also that a sizeable number of students were missing more than 20% of school days in a year (about 36 days), especially in high school. **Figure 2** shows this breakdown for sixth and ninth grade; other grades showed similar patterns. While it was rare for sixth-grade students to be absent 20% or more before the pandemic, 8% of students were absent this much in the 2023-24 school year. In the ninth grade, over one-fifth of students were absent 20% or more. In addition, there were fewer students with strong attendance (missing less than 5% of school days). Two-thirds of sixth-graders and almost one-half of ninth-graders missed less than 5% of school days (about 9 days) before the pandemic, but in the 2023-24 school year, only 44% of sixth-graders and 30% of ninth-graders missed less than 5%. While some students maintained strong attendance habits, a growing number were missing substantial portions of school. This is a troubling pattern, since attendance continues to be a strong predictor of education success, as it was before the pandemic.

FIGURE 2

More students were very chronically absent, and fewer students missed less than 5% of school days, in SY22-24 relative to SY17-19

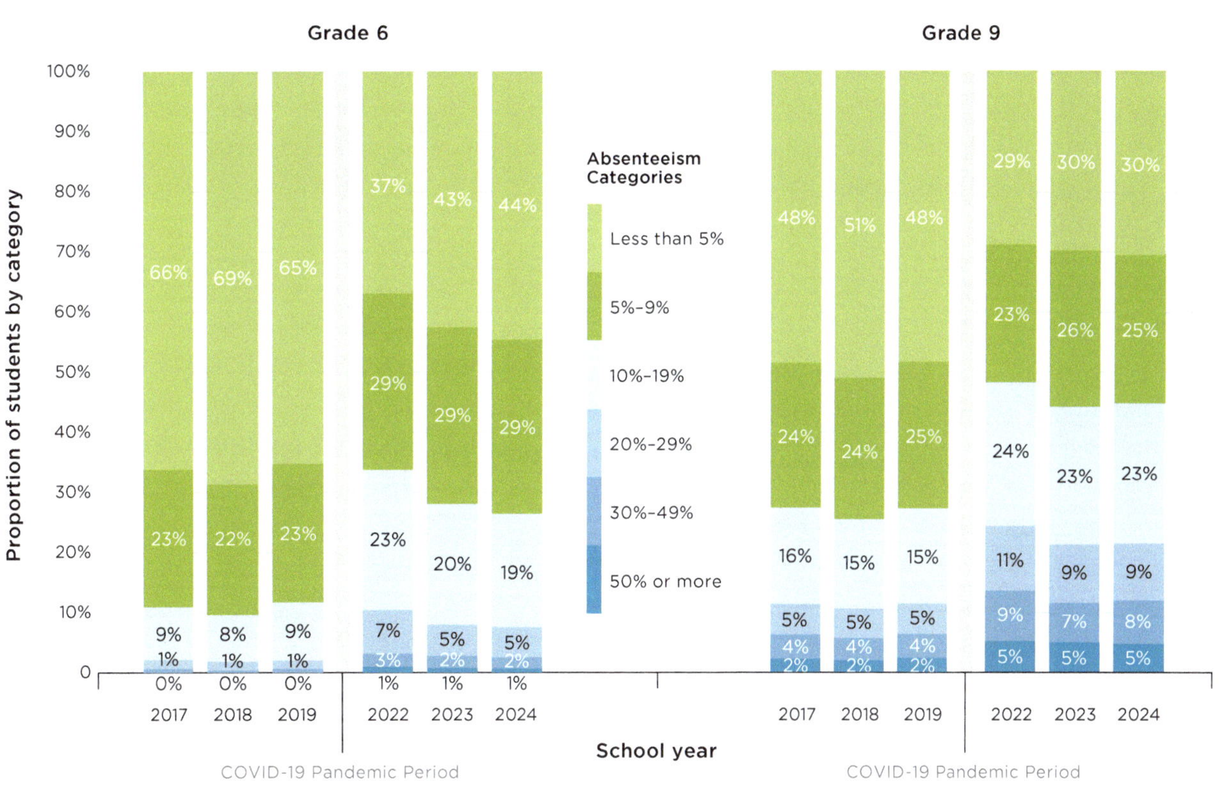

Note: Absenteeism categories reflect the proportion of students in each absenteeism category. These categories are based on the annual absence rates, which are defined as the number of days a student missed school in an academic year, divided by the number of days enrolled. Years represent the spring of the academic year.

Key Finding 02

Research Question 2

Students' academic achievement continued to be as strongly related to their absences in post-pandemic years as in pre-pandemic years

Middle grade and high school students who had lower absences had higher test scores and GPAs in both pre- and post-pandemic years. In post-pandemic years, the correlations of absences with standardized test scores ranged from -0.29 to -0.36 across the grade levels, while the correlations of absences with GPAs ranged from -0.41 to -0.68. These correlations were somewhat larger than in pre-pandemic years. **Figures 3 and 4** show the general patterns using sixth and ninth grade as examples. Differences from these patterns at other grades are described in the text, while tables and figures showing all grades are available in the Technical Appendix. Absences also showed similar relationships with test-score gains in both periods, with details available in the Technical Appendix.

Figure 3 shows the relationship between absence rates and test scores by displaying the average test scores for sixth- and ninth-graders with different absence rates in the pre- and post-pandemic years. The average test scores were almost identical in post-pandemic years as pre-pandemic years in these grades. For example, the difference in average Illinois Assessment of Readiness (IAR) test scores for sixth-graders who missed 10% of days relative to those who missed no days of school (at the far left of the regression line) was about 16 points in both pre-pandemic years (732 to 716) and in post-pandemic years (734 to 718). A difference of 16 points is about one-half of a standard deviation on the IAR, which is similar to the difference between scores at the 50th vs. the 30th percentile.[10] **At the high school level, like the middle grades, the relationships also looked the same in pre- and post-pandemic years.** This can be seen in the right-hand panel of Figure 3 for ninth grade.

In grades 7-8 (not shown here, but available in the Technical Appendix), the relationships, as demonstrated by the slopes of the lines, were the same, so the change in test score for each increase in absence rates was the same. However, students at all absence levels had slightly higher test scores in post-pandemic years than in pre-pandemic years in grades 7-8. This phenomenon also occurred with GPAs and is discussed further.

10 The sixth-grade IAR has a standard deviation of 33.87 in grade 6, based on Pearson (2024).

FIGURE 3

Students with higher absence rates had lower test scores in both pre- and post-pandemic years

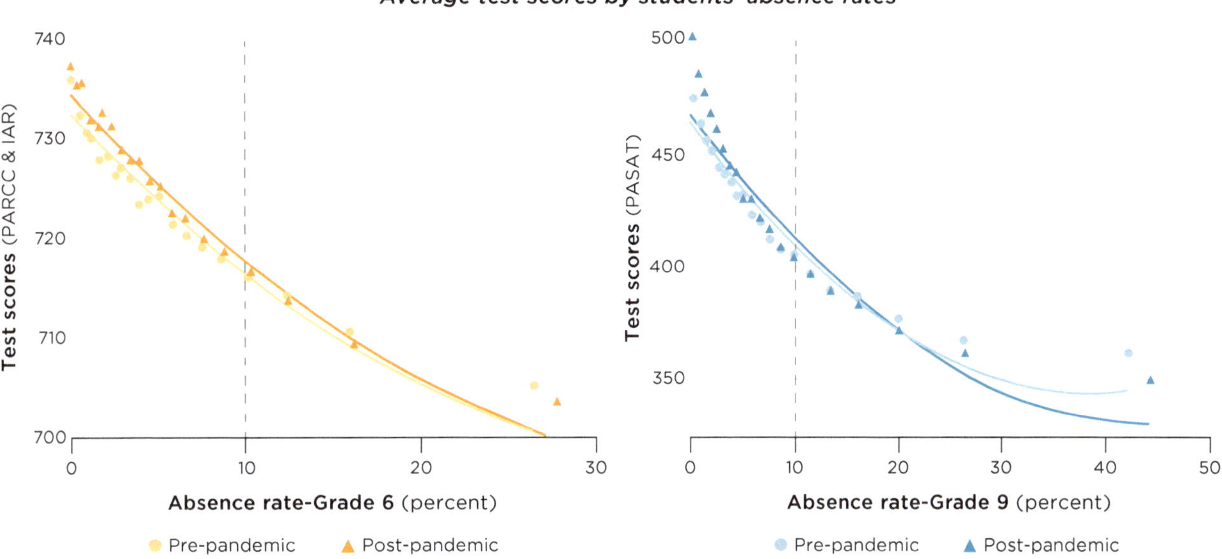

Note: Partnership for Assessment of Readiness for College and Careers (PARCC) and IAR are standardized tests given to students in grades 3-8 in Illinois. Beginning in the 2018-19 school year, Illinois used a modified version of the PARCC, called the IAR, with both tests are on the same scale. PSAT and SAT are standardized tests given to students in grades 9-10 (PSAT) and 11 (SAT). Each dot represents a group of students with similar absence rates and their average test scores in English and math combined. The lines are modeled with linear and quadratic terms. Pre-pandemic lines represent SY17-19; post-pandemic lines represent SY22-24. The dashed line indicates the point at which students are chronically absent (missing 10% of school days).

Figure 4 shows the relationship between absence rates and students' GPAs in each period for sixth and ninth grade. The slope of the relationships between absence rates and GPAs was similar in post-pandemic years as in pre-pandemic years. For example, the difference in average GPAs for sixth-graders who were absent 10% of days, relative to those who missed no days, was about 0.4 GPA points in both pre-pandemic years (3.3 to 2.9) and post-pandemic years (3.6 to 3.2). However, the lines were not on top of each other because students with the same level of absences had higher grades in post-pandemic years than students with the same absences pre-pandemic. For example, sixth-graders with absence rates of 10% had average GPAs of 2.9 in pre-pandemic years while students with the same absence rates had average GPAs of 3.2 in post-pandemic years.

The increase in GPAs in post-pandemic years, relative to students with the same absence rates in pre-pandemic years, is observed at all grade levels. The fact that students in post-pandemic years had higher GPAs, and in grades 7-8 had higher standardized test scores than students with similar attendance in pre-pandemic years deserves further study. There are a number of potential explanations. For example, technology may have influenced students' ability to receive and turn in assignments, communicate with teachers, or to complete assignments and quizzes, grading practices or standards may have changed, and testing conditions may have changed. Looking into all these potential changes is beyond the scope of the current study, but is important to recognize to contextualize the findings. **Achievement levels were not the same as before the pandemic, but higher absence rates were associated with lower levels of achievement in all years.**

FIGURE 4

Students with higher absence rates had lower GPAs than students with lower absence rates in both pre- and post-pandemic years, but students at all absence levels had higher GPAs in post-pandemic years.

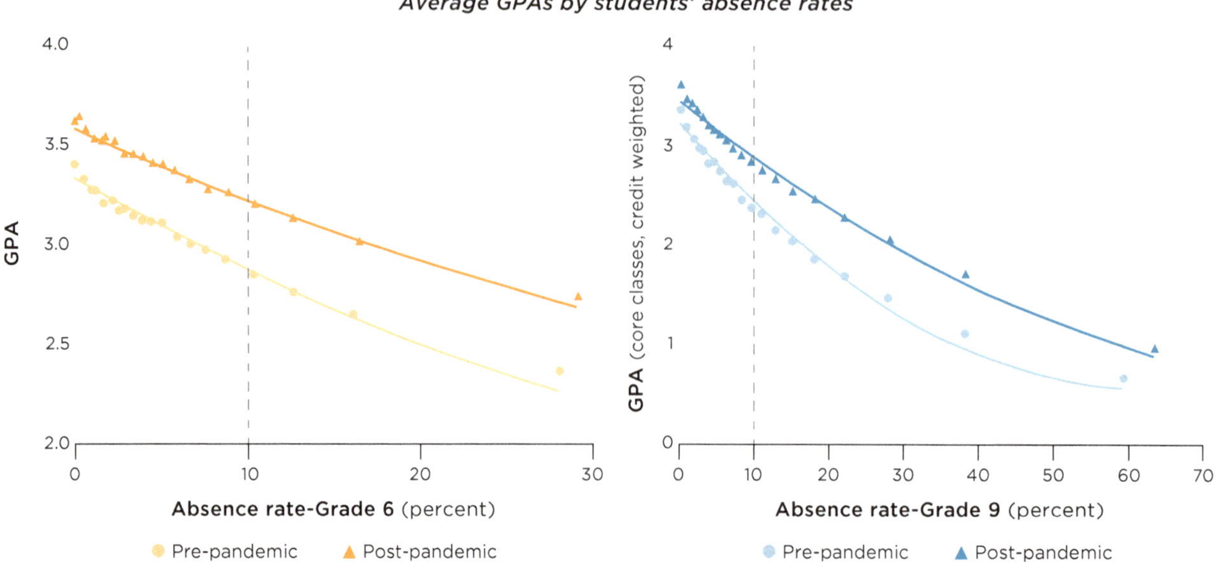

Note: Each dot represents a group of students with similar absence rates and their average GPA, which is the average GPA of all the courses taken that year in the middle grades and core courses (English, math, science, and social studies) in high school. Pre-pandemic lines represent SY17-19; post-pandemic lines represent SY22-24. The dashed line indicates the point at which students are chronically absent (missing 10% of school days).

Notably, across all achievement indicators (test scores, GPAs, and test gains), the degree of absence matters, not just at the 10% mark which indicates a student is chronically absent. Achievement was lower with each greater increment of absence for both chronically and non-chronically absent students. Fewer absences were associated with higher achievement, regardless of whether students' overall absence rates were low or high.

Key Finding 03

Research Question 3

Schools serving similar students from similar neighborhoods often had differing absence rates

While absenteeism rose across the district, the increase in absenteeism was not the same across all schools, suggesting that some schools may have used strategies that were more effective for maintaining attendance during this time period. Schools varied considerably in how much their absence rates changed after the pandemic. **Figure 5** shows absence rates before (x-axis) and after the pandemic (y-axis); each dot is a school. The rates shown do not control for differences in the students served by the school, but compare schools to themselves in years before and after the pandemic to descriptively show what happened to absence rates by school. Schools positioned above the diagonal line experienced higher absenteeism in the post-pandemic years, with those further above the line showing the largest increases. Those dots located on the diagonal line, or below it, did not show increases in absence rates. Notably, there was no uniform experience across schools—while most saw higher absenteeism, some showed little or no change in their absence rates. This was true for both middle grades and high schools. It was also true for schools that started out with low or high absence rates—among schools at all levels of absence pre-pandemic, some showed large increases in absence rates in the post-pandemic years while others showed little or no increase.

FIGURE 5

Schools varied considerably in the extent to which absenteeism increased after the pandemic

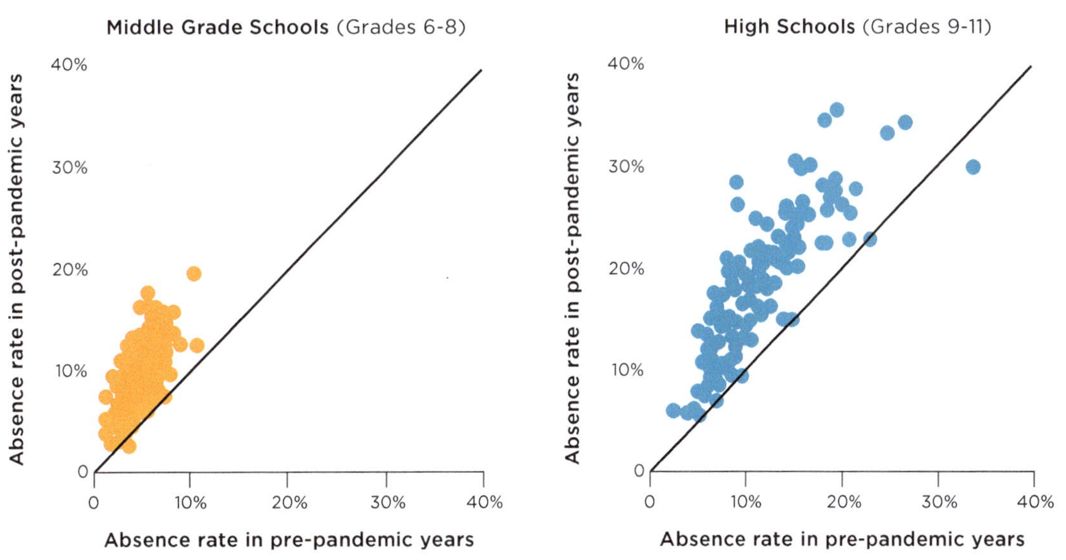

Note: Each dot represents one school. Points on the diagonal line are schools with no change in absence rates after the pandemic. Dots above the line are schools that had higher absence rates after the pandemic than before the pandemic. The further the dot is above the diagonal line, the larger the change in absence rates in that school after the pandemic. These figures are descriptive and do not control for differences in the students served by the schools. There are 464 schools serving the middle grades and 128 schools serving high school grades represented.

Differences among schools' absence rates also became larger in post-pandemic years. To put these differences in context, we compare schools at the 75th percentile to those at the 25th percentile, using the estimated variation from a model that takes into account the school students attended. In pre-pandemic years, schools at the 75th percentile had absence rates that were 1.8 percentage points higher than schools at the 25th percentile in pre-pandemic years in the middle grades. This nearly doubled to 3.2 points after the pandemic. Differences for high schools were much larger than middle schools with a 7.6 point difference between schools at the 25th and 75th percentiles before the pandemic, increasing to 9.2 after the pandemic.

Differences in schools' absence rates could represent differences in neighborhood characteristics where students reside.[11] For example, students living in neighborhoods with higher crime rates, limited transportation availability, and economic instability face structural barriers to regular school attendance that are independent of school efforts. Therefore, we conducted statistical analyses that adjusted school absence rates for differences attributable to the neighborhood in which students lived.[12] Within the same neighborhood, students faced different obstacles to attending school, such as family obligations and health issues. While we cannot know all the potential barriers that individual students faced, it is likely that many students who faced barriers in the middle and high school grades also faced barriers when they were in earlier grades. Therefore, we also look at the degree to which students' absences changed in the middle and high school grades, relative to students' absences in earlier years, and we consider other information on student background that might be related to their absences. **Table 1** displays the differences in school absences without considering neighborhood or background factors in column 1, after taking into account neighborhood factors in column 2, and after taking into account students' neighborhoods, prior absence rates, and backgrounds in column 3.

School variation did not change much when we took into account the neighborhood where students resided, either before or after the pandemic. This suggests the school students attended affected their attendance much more than the neighborhood in which they lived. The differences in absence rates for schools at the 25th and 75th percentiles were similar in column 2 of Table 1, which takes into account differences in absence rates by students' neighborhood, relative to the rates that do not take other factors into account shown in column 1. In the middle grades, the differences at the 75th vs. 25th percentiles were 3.0 points in post-pandemic years, after taking into account students' residential neighborhood, compared to 3.2 points, without consideration of their neighborhood. Among high schools, absence rates between the 25th and 75th percentiles were different by 8.7 points, after taking into account students' residential neighborhood, compared to 9.2 points, without considering their neighborhood. (**See the Technical Appendix for more details on the analysis**).

11 Chicago is a choice district where students may apply to schools and programs throughout the city through a centralized enrollment system that takes into account criteria at selective schools, and conducts lotteries for over-subscribed non-selective schools (Barrow & Sartain, 2019). In 2024, approximately 49% of CPS students in the middle grades and 83% of high school students attended a school other than their attendance-area school.

12 Neighborhoods in this analysis were represented by census tracts. Chicago is divided into 866 census tracts.

After the pandemic, school differences narrowed when student characteristics and prior absences were taken into account, but differences among schools remained significant. Note that we likely underestimate the true effects schools had on attendance with these estimates, especially in the middle grades; many schools served grades K-8, and if school strategies in grades 3-5 were similar to those in grades 6-8, we would control those out by adjusting for students' attendance in prior years.[13] However, there were still significant differences between schools in absence rates (**see the rightmost column in Table 1**). At the high school level, schools at the 75th percentile had absence rates that were 5.9 points higher than schools at the 25th percentile, after controlling for their students' absences in prior years and backgrounds. That's about 10 days of school. In the middle grades, the differences between the 25th and 75th percentiles were modest, after taking into account students' prior absences and backgrounds, differing by 1.8 points in post-pandemic years, which is 3.2 days. Yet, remember that this controls for differences in students' average attendance in grades 3-5, which likely leads to an underestimate of school effects for schools serving grades K-8.

Thus, differences in students' background characteristics and prior attendance accounted for some of the differences across schools in their absence rates, reflecting unique challenges faced by individual students. At the same time, over one-half of the variation in absences by school were not associated with students' prior absences or backgrounds (compare Table 1, column 1 to column 3). **Schools serving similar students coming from similar neighborhoods had very different absence rates.**

Next, we explore some of those potential factors, specifically looking at the role of school climate.

TABLE 1

Similar students from similar neighborhoods had different absence rates at different schools

School differences in average absence rates from HLM models: school at 75th vs 25th percentile

		No Controls	Considering Residential Neighborhood	Considering Residential Neighborhood and Controlling Student Backgrounds
Grades 6-8	**Pre-Pandemic**	1.8 ppt	1.8 ppt	1.5ppt
	Post-Pandemic	3.2 ppt	3.0 ppt	1.8ppt
Grades 9-11	**Pre-Pandemic**	7.6 ppt	7.3 ppt	5.2ppt
	Post-Pandemic	9.2 ppt	8.7 ppt	5.9ppt

Note: Pre-pandemic years include 2017 to 2019, while post-pandemic years are 2022 to 2024. Differences shown in the first column come from school variance components out of unconditional hierarchical linear models (HLM) with students nested in schools, translated to percentile based on the estimated school-level variance. The second column is based on school variance from cross-nested HLMs with students nested simultaneously in their school and residential neighborhoods depicted by their census tract, and no other covariates. The third column comes from cross-nested models that incorporate student demographic and socioeconomic variables, as well as students' prior attendance and prior test scores in earlier grades. See the Technical Appendix for a more detailed description. Models are run separately by pandemic period, so the resulting estimates of school effects in column 3 allow for student characteristics to have different relationships with absences in post-pandemic years.

13 To isolate school effects on absences, we removed differences in school absence rates that could be attributed to the backgrounds of their students across a wide array of factors, including students' average achievement (grades 3-5 in middle grades analysis and grades 6-8 in high school grades analysis), race, ethnicity, Individualized Education Plan (IEP) and English Learner (EL) status, temporary living situation, and economic characteristics of their census block group. Importantly, when analyzing middle grade absence rates, we accounted for students' prior absence rates when students were in grades 3-5, and when analyzing high school absence rates, we accounted for students' prior absences when they were in grades 6-8. By doing this, we created measures that reflect how much student absence rates change during middle school or high school, compared to their prior attendance history.

Key Finding 04

Research Question 4

Many dimensions of school climate were associated with lower school absences, especially in post-pandemic years

Prior research shows that school climate measures are powerful predictors of student attendance patterns, as students' perceptions of their school directly influence their motivation to attend. Safety, relationships with peers and teachers, and parent engagement in schools are some of those dimensions of school climate that have shown relationships with attendance.[14] We used reports of students and teachers on the *5Essentials* school climate survey to see if school differences in climate coincided with the differences in school absence rates not attributable to student backgrounds, prior attendance, and residential neighborhood. Descriptions of each measure included in the analysis are in the **Technical Appendix, Table A.5**.

As shown in **Figure 6**, school differences in absence rates were related to student and teacher reports about their experiences in their school. **In fact, school climate was even more strongly related to absenteeism after the pandemic than before.**[15] This is indicated by the length of each of the bars which represent a difference of 1.35 standard deviations, which corresponds to the difference between the 25th and 75th percentiles. The more the bar extends to the left, the bigger the difference in absence rates between schools at the 75th percentile on that aspect of school climate and schools at the 25th percentile. The scales are different for high schools than middle schools in terms of percentage points, but they represent the same amount of variability in school absence rates since high schools differ from each other much more than schools serving the middle grades.[16]

Students' reports of feeling safe at school showed some of the strongest relationships with absences (Related survey measures: safety in/around the school and safety from bullying/teasing), especially in high schools, providing evidence that feeling unsafe, whether bullying or other type of violence, discourages attending school. In high schools, adjusted absence rates were about 4 percentage points lower in schools with strong versus weak safety after the pandemic, compared to a difference of about 1 percentage point before the pandemic. In the middle grades, the differences were about half of a percentage point, which was statistically significant even if it seems small.

---

14 Hart Young, Chen, Zou, & Allensworth (2020); Malcolm, Wilson, Davidson, & Kirk (2003); Sheldon & Epstein (2004).

15 The stronger relationships could partially be a consequence of larger differences in school absence rates after the pandemic. The standard deviations of school absence rates were 1.35 after the pandemic and 1.13 before the pandemic in the middle grades and 4.39 after the pandemic and 3.82 before the pandemic in high schools, after controlling for differences in student population in the schools.

16 The estimated standard deviation for middle school post pandemic with student covariates was 1.35 and 4.39 for high schools (see Table A.4 in the Technical Appendix) Therefore, the scale represented in the graphs is roughly 1.3 standard deviations.

Attendance was higher in schools where students' relationships with their peers and teachers were stronger. Likewise, in schools where more students felt disconnected from their school or not valued or supported by teachers and peers attendance was lower. Students' reports of connectedness to school were particularly strongly related to absences in post-pandemic years for high school students, although it was not significantly related to absences before the pandemic. *Related survey measures: student peer relationships, school connectedness, peer support for academic work, academic personalism, and student-teacher trust at the middle grade level.*

There is also evidence that the degree to which students find value and meaning in their classes influences their attendance. Students' reports on how academically demanding their classes were showed a relationship with absences; higher levels on these measures were related to lower absence rates in middle and high school grades. The academic engagement in their classes was related to absences in middle grade schools but not in high schools. *Related survey measures: academic press and also academic engagement in middle school.*

Teachers' reports of their relationships with parents were also significantly related to absence rates in their school in both middle grades and high schools. Developing stronger connections between parents and schools perhaps made parents feel welcome in schools and gain access to resources, and improve communications, to help ensure their children attend regularly. Again, the relationships were even stronger in post-pandemic years than before the pandemic. Unlike other barriers, such as transportation or health issues, that schools cannot directly control, school environment is something that practitioners can actively work to improve. *Related survey measures: teacher-parent trust, parent involvement in school and parent influence on decision making.*

FIGURE 6

Many dimensions of school culture and climate were related to absenteeism, especially after the pandemic

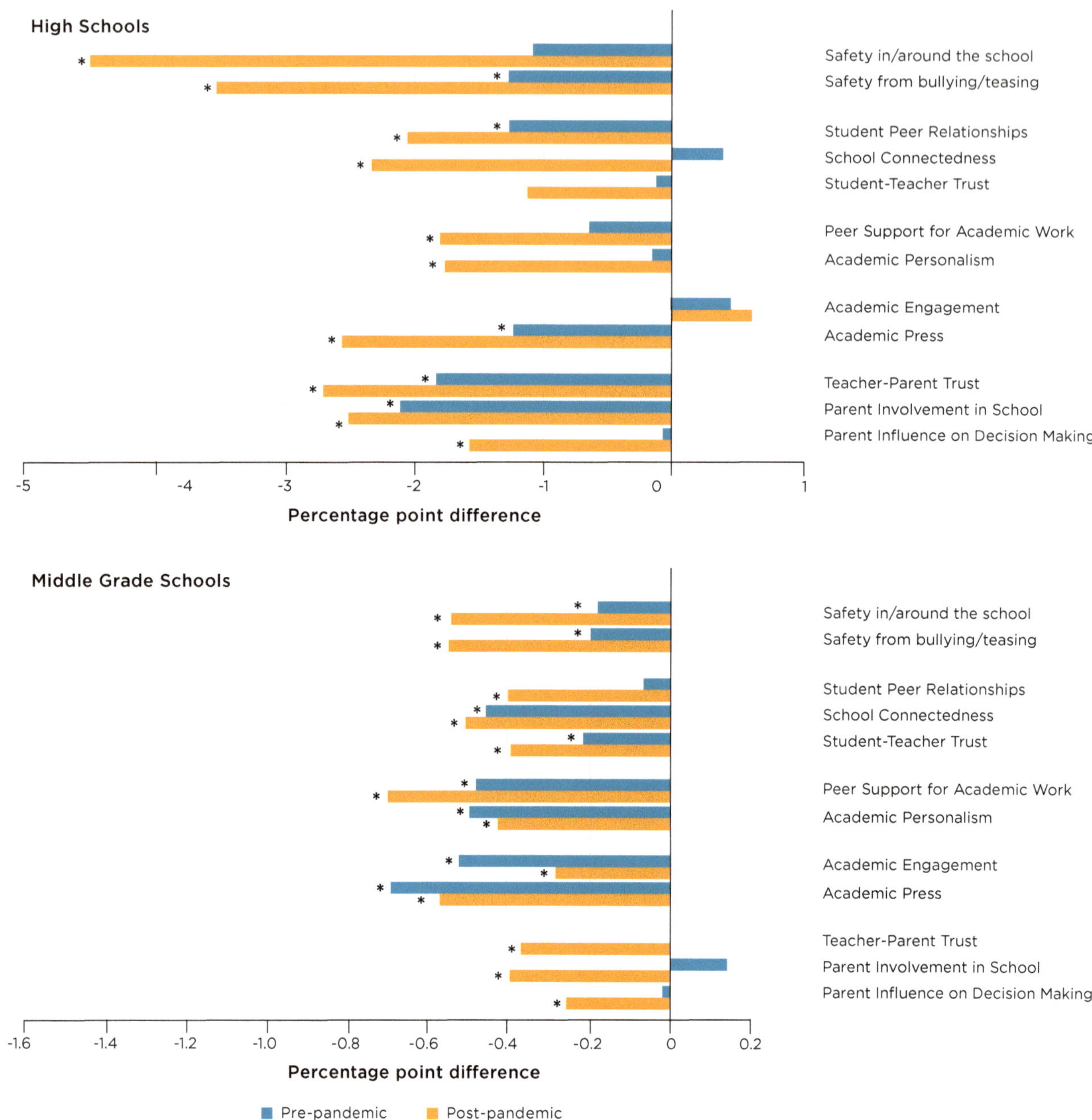

Note: Bars indicate a 1.35 standard deviation difference based on variance components from HLM models, which corresponds to the difference between schools at the 25th and 75th percentiles on the climate measure. Based on cross-nested hierarchical linear models with students nested simultaneously in their schools and census tracts that account for students' baseline average absences and standardized test scores in grades 3-5 (when predicting absences in the middle grades) or grades 6-8 (when predicting absences in high school), students' demographic characteristics (race, ethnicity, gender), their specific IEP designation, whether they were an English Learner, whether they attended their neighborhood school, whether they were in temporary living situations, grade level, and indicators of income and social status in their residential census block group (percent of families under the poverty line, male unemployment rates, median family income, and average education level of adults over age 25). There is no bar for teacher-parent trust in the middle grades in pre-pandemic years because the relationship with attendance is very close to zero.

* Statistical significance of the relationship between the school measure and school absences at the 0.05 level.

Interpretive Summary and Next Steps

This study demonstrates that **attendance matters as much as ever** for students' grades and test scores, and gains on standardized tests. The more students are present, the more they can learn; and the more they're absent, the more their grades and test scores drop. The persistence of increased rates of chronic absenteeism following the COVID-19 pandemic threatens to undermine the hard-fought gains in student achievement that occurred prior to the pandemic.

Our analysis showing that schools serving similar students from similar neighborhoods can have very different absence rates strongly suggests that **schools can influence the degree to which students are absent** from school, if they know what to focus on and have the resources needed. There are many different strategies that can support better attendance, including clear communication about the importance of attendance, a welcoming environment promoted by all school staff, rigorous and engaging classroom environments, and specialized supports for students facing particularly difficult barriers. Jordan (2023) summarizes a range of strategies that schools have used to reduce absenteeism. Given the connection between a school's *5Essentials* Survey data and attendance, schools can use their survey data to better understand areas where they could better support **1)** students' experiences in school, and **2)** teachers' relationships with parents, and work in collaboration with students and parents to improve them.

Improving school climate takes time and sustained effort; it's about real, felt changes in the school, not just higher numbers on survey reports. But this research adds to the growing body of evidence showing that **improving school climate is one of the most effective ways to improve student achievement and students' long-term outcomes.**[17] In other studies, researchers found that school climate itself is malleable, meaning it can change over time.[18] And changes in students' reports from one year to the next are associated with improvements in student outcomes, including attendance.[19] It also suggests that schools working to improve absenteeism might need to pay more attention to many elements of students' experiences than they did before the pandemic.

While these findings underscore the ability of schools to influence student attendance, it is also important to acknowledge that schools alone are neither the cause nor the solution to increases in chronic absenteeism rates. Students' attendance is affected by many things outside of school, and while school practices can, and do, make a big difference, school staff cannot shoulder the role of supporting students and families alone. This study does not address the barriers that schools face implementing strong practices, the resources they need, or the specific practices that are most effective.

17 Hart et. al. (2020), Jackson, Kiguel, Porter, & Easton (2024).
18 Young & Hart (2025).
19 Hart et. al. (2020).

To help schools focus their efforts on where they can have the most impact, our next phase of this mixed-methods study is investigating a broad range of school, neighborhood, and individual factors affecting absenteeism to understand where supports could have the largest impacts, addressing such questions as:

- **How are student-specific and community-level factors related to attendance in post-pandemic years?** We will bring student and neighborhood data on factors that likely influence student attendance, such as students' mode of transportation to school, chronic illness, health insurance rates, housing instability, and COVID-19 and flu case rates in students' residential areas.
- **Which resources differentiate schools with larger effects on attendance?** Because we have shown that schools can influence student attendance, we will expand the analysis to understand whether resources measured by things such as creative schools' certifications, school's status on supporting health and well-being of students (Healthy CPS badges), sustainable community school status, and access to green spaces, differentiate schools with larger effects on attendance.
- **What are the practices and policies at schools with stronger-than expected attendance?** We'll interview staff at these schools and then speak with students and families to learn their perspectives.

References

Allensworth, E., de la Torre, M., Franklin, K., & Xu, J. (2025)
Identifying indicators to support educational attainment for different groups of English learners in high school. (EdWorkingPaper: 25-1241). Annenberg Institute at Brown University. https://doi.org/10.26300/yf35-e829

Allensworth, E.M., Gwynne, J.A., Moore, P., & de la Torre, M. (2014)
Looking forward to high school and college: Middle grade indicators of readiness in chicago public schools. Chicago, IL: University of Chicago Consortium on Chicago School Research.

Allensworth, E., & Easton, J.Q. (2007)
What matters for staying on-track and graduating in Chicago Public Schools. Chicago, IL: University of Chicago Consortium on Chicago School Research.

Attendance Works & Healthy Schools Campaign. (2015)
Mapping the early attendance gap: Charting a course for school success. San Francisco, CA: Attendance Works.

Attendance Works. (2025, November 20)
Why are so many students missing so much school? Attendance Works. https://www.attendanceworks.org/resources/toolkits/teaching-attendance-2-0/use-data-for-intervention-and-support/strategy-2-consider-needed-supports/why-are-so-many-students-missing-so-much-school/

Aucejo, E.M., & Romano, T.F. (2016)
Assessing the effect of school days and absences on test score performance. *Economics of Education Review, 55*, 70-87.

Barrow, L., & Sartain, L. (2019)
GoCPS: A first look at ninth-grade applications, offers, and enrollment. Chicago, IL: University of Chicago Consortium on School Research.

Barshay, J. (2025, August 4)
7 insights about chronic absenteeism, a new normal for American schools, *The Hechinger Report.* https://hechingerreport.org/proof-points-7-insights-chronic-absenteeism/

Forrest, C.B., Bevans, K.B., Riley, A.W., Crespo, R., & Louis, T.A. (2011)
School outcomes of children with special health care needs. *Pediatrics, 128*(2), 303–312.

Garcia, E., & Weiss, E. (2018)
Student absenteeism: Who, what, and why. Washington, DC: Economic Policy Institute.

Gottfried, M.A. (2014)
Chronic absenteeism and its effects on students' academic and socioemotional outcomes. *Journal of Education for Students Placed at Risk, 19*(2), 53–75.

Hart, H., Young, C., Chen, A., Zou, A., & Allensworth, E.M. (2020)
Supporting school improvement: Early findings from reexamination of the 5Essentials *survey.* Chicago, IL: University of Chicago Consortium on School Research.

Jackson, C.K., Kiguel, S., Porter, S.C., & Easton, J.Q. (2024)
Who benefits from attending effective high schools? *Journal of Labor Economics, 42*(3), 717-751.

Jordan, P. (2023)
Attendance playbook: Smart strategies for reducing student absenteeism post-pandemic. Washington, DC: FutureEd and Attendance Works.

Kirksey, J.J. (2019)
Academic harms of missing high school and the accuracy of current policy thresholds: Analysis of preregistered administrative data from a California school district. *AERA Open, 5*(3), 1-13.

Malcolm, H., Wilson, V., Davidson, J., & Kirk, S. (2003)
Absence from school: A study of its causes and effects in seven LEAs. Glasgow, Scotland: The SCRE Centre University of Glasgow.

Malkus, N. (2025)
Lingering absence in public schools tracking post-pandemic chronic absenteeism into 2024. Washington, DC: American Enterprise Institute.

Pearson (2024)
Illinois Assessment of Readiness (IAR) technical report, 2023–2024. London, England: Pearson Education.

Ready, D.D. (2010)
Socioeconomic disadvantage, school attendance, and early cognitive development: The differential effects of school exposure. *Sociology of Education, 83*(4), 271-286.

Schmid, H. (2023, January 30)
Nearly half of Chicago Public Schools students chronically absent in 2022. Illinois Policy. https://www.illinoispolicy.org/nearly-half-of-chicago-public-schools-students-chronically-absent-in-2022/

Sheldon, S.B., & Epstein, J.L. (2004)
Getting students to school: Using family and community involvement to reduce chronic absenteeism. *School Community Journal, 14*(2), 39-56.

Young, C., & Hart, H. (2025)
The malleability of school climate: Lessons from the 5Essentials *Survey in Chicago Public Schools.* Chicago, IL: University of Chicago Consortium on School Research.

Technical Appendix

Connection, Trust, and Learning

Student Attendance in the Middle and High School Grades Following the COVID-19 Pandemic

Data

The data come from Chicago Public Schools (CPS) administrative data files that contain data on:

- The number of days a student was absent
- The number of days a student was enrolled
- Standardized test scores: PARCC and IAR for middle grade students and PSAT and SAT for high school students
- Course grades
- Demographic information
- Census tract where student resided
- Data from the annual *5Essentials* Surveys of students and teachers.

We also use publicly available census data at the tract level to calculate measures of poverty and social status.

Absence rate is calculated as the number of days a student missed in a school year divided by the number of days enrolled.

Sample selection

The analyses included students in grades 6-11 in CPS in school years 2016–17, 2017–18, 2018–19, 2021–22, 2022–23, and 2023–24. We omitted the 2019–20 and 2020–21 school years because of the disruptions of the COVID-19 pandemic, when instruction for part, or all, of the school year was virtual or hybrid. Students who transferred during the school year are included with their first school.

Our initial sample includes all active middle and high school students (grades 6 -12). Almost all students in the sample (98.8%) have attendance data, leaving us with 1,091,091 observations. We perform the following additional sample restrictions:

- We include students with a minimum enrollment of 20 days for the entire year, aligned with how CPS collects student enrollment data on the 20th day (0.34% of observations dropped). This differs from the CPS inclusion rule which includes students with a minimum of 11 days of enrollment for the year, resulting in slightly different numbers from those produced by the district.
- We exclude school-grades that have fewer than 10 students. (0.19% dropped)
- We exclude students in fully remote academies, Options schools, and alternative schools (4.75% dropped). Students in charter schools are included in all analyses except for the analysis of the relationship between attendance and GPAs. Analysis of students' GPAs does not include students in charter schools as their transcript data are not collected centrally.
- We also exclude students from grade 12 for the analyses (12.80% dropped), because we learned that they could be counted as absent in the final weeks of school when they were no longer required to attend after their graduation. This inaccurately inflates absence rates for twelfth-graders.

After sample restrictions and excluding twelfth-graders, our main analytic sample consists of 901,290 observations (all students in grades 6-11 in each year studied, with students included as an observation for each year they were in one of the included grades). **Table A.1** presents descriptive statistics for middle and high school students separately for pre- and post-pandemic years.

Table A.1 Descriptive statistics of the analytic sample

	Middle school students (Grades 6-8)				High school students (Grades 9-11)			
	Pre-pandemic years (2016–17 to 2018–19)		Post-pandemic years (2021–22 to 2023–24)		Pre-pandemic years (2016–17 to 2018–19)		Post-pandemic years (2021–22 to 2023–24)	
	N/mean	%/sd	N/mean	%/sd	N/mean	%/sd	N/mean	%/sd
Demographics								
Female	0.495	(0.500)	0.493	(0.500)	0.503	(0.500)	0.502	(0.500)
White	0.099	(0.299)	0.106	(0.308)	0.091	(0.288)	0.098	(0.298)
Black	0.360	(0.480)	0.359	(0.480)	0.365	(0.481)	0.339	(0.473)
Latinx	0.486	(0.500)	0.475	(0.499)	0.487	(0.500)	0.504	(0.500)
Asian	0.039	(0.193)	0.043	(0.203)	0.042	(0.201)	0.043	(0.204)
Free/reduced-price lunch	0.825	(0.380)	0.778	(0.416)	0.815	(0.388)	0.769	(0.422)
Special education	0.158	(0.365)	0.159	(0.366)	0.150	(0.357)	0.153	(0.360)
English Learner	0.115	(0.319)	0.218	(0.413)	0.094	(0.292)	0.178	(0.382)
Attendance								
Attendance rate	95.155	(5.886)	91.176	(9.174)	89.815	(12.544)	83.634	(17.292)
Absence rate	4.845	(5.886)	8.824	(9.174)	10.185	(12.544)	16.366	(17.292)
Chronically absent	0.110	(0.313)	0.298	(0.457)	0.313	(0.464)	0.510	(0.500)
Academic								
GPA MS	3.126	(0.661)	3.276	(0.591)				
GPA HS (core courses, credit weighted)					2.543	(0.996)	2.653	(1.023)
Avg math and English PARCC scores	726.250	(31.220)						
Avg math and English IAR scores	725.324	(31.642)	723.979	(31.660)				
Avg math and English PSAT scores					438.324	(87.787)	421.144	(94.336)
Avg math and English SAT scores					482.285	(94.984)	460.534	(101.655)
N	241,928	(26.8%)	214,299	(23.8%)	227,261	(25.2%)	217,802	(24.2%)

Additional information on Key Finding 2

Academic achievement continues to be strongly related to students' absences in post-pandemic years

The sections below show the relationships of absences with achievement for all grades, as well as the relationships of absences with test score gains.

Relationships of achievement with standardized test scores for all grades

Table A.2 shows that there were moderately-sized correlations of absence rates with test scores in both post-pandemic and pre-pandemic years at each grade level, and moderate-to-strong relationships of absences with GPAs. The correlations were larger after the pandemic than before the pandemic. This occurred because there were more students with high absence rates in post-pandemic years, allowing the relationship between high absence rates and achievement to be defined more clearly than when few students had very high absence rates. Correlations measure how closely two variables move together, so they can increase when there is more variation in one of the variables, making patterns between the two variables clearer.

Table A.2 Correlations of absences with achievement

Grade	Test Score Pre-Pandemic	Test Score Post-Pandemic	GPA Pre-Pandemic	GPA Post-Pandemic
6	-0.21	-0.29	-0.30	-0.41
7	-0.22	-0.29	-0.33	-0.43
8	-0.19	-0.26	-0.33	-0.43
9	-0.31	-0.33	-0.59	-0.65
10	-0.30	-0.35	-0.58	-0.68
11	-0.29	-0.36	-0.56	-0.67

Note: Correlations show the strength of the relationship between two variables and range from -1 to 1, where 0 means no relationship and 1 indicates the strongest possible positive relationship, while -1 indicates the strongest possible negative relationship (where achievement goes down when absences go up).

The slope (regression coefficient) shows how much one variable changes when the other changes; it can be smaller even if the overall correlation is stronger, because it is based on a broader range of values. The bivariate regression coefficients representing the slope (change in achievement per change in absence rate) are not larger in post-pandemic years, and in some cases are smaller than in pre-pandemic years, as shown in **Table A.3**.

Table A.3. Bivariate regressions of achievement on absences

Grade	Test Score Pre-Pandemic	Test Score Post-Pandemic	GPA Pre-Pandemic	GPA Post-Pandemic
6	-1.26	-1.10	-0.04	-0.03
7	-1.35	-1.06	-0.04	-0.03
8	-1.24	-1.15	-0.04	-0.03
9	-3.14	-2.81	-0.05	-0.04
10	-2.97	-2.49	-0.05	-0.04
11	-2.82	-2.54	-0.05	-0.04

Note: Table shows bivariate regression coefficients after regressing test scores (in raw scores) or GPA on absence rates.

The figures in the main report show relationships between students' absences and achievement descriptively, grouping student absence rates into 20 equally-size groups, and then calculating the average achievement level of the different indicators for students in those groups, as well as a regression line that provides the best fit for the points using a quadratic model. The main report focuses on grades six and nine. **Figure A.1** shows the relationships of absence with test scores for all grades, while **Figure A.2** shows the relationships between absences and GPAs. All analyses of GPA data do not include charter school students.

The patterns are similar to those for grades six and nine. The relationships show similar slopes in pre- and post-pandemic years, indicating the strength of the relationships are the same. Yet, the average GPAs are higher in post-pandemic years for students with the same absence rates. One difference from grades six and nine is that in grades seven and eight, test scores in post-pandemic years were also higher than in pre-pandemic years for students with the same absence rates.

Figure A.1 Students with higher absence rates had lower test scores in all grades

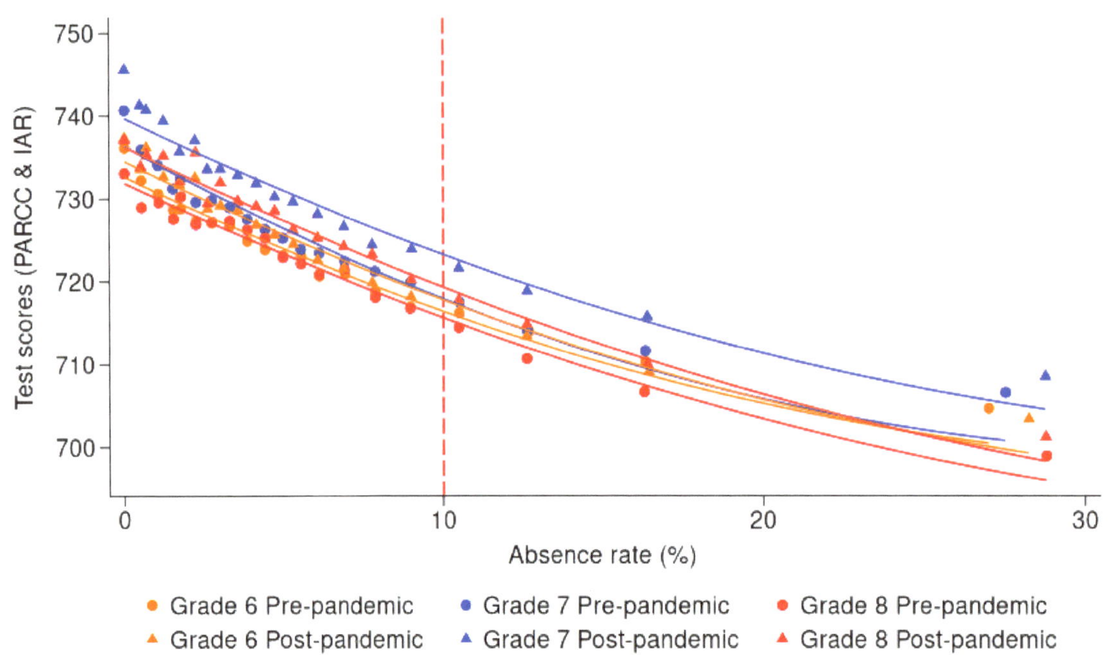

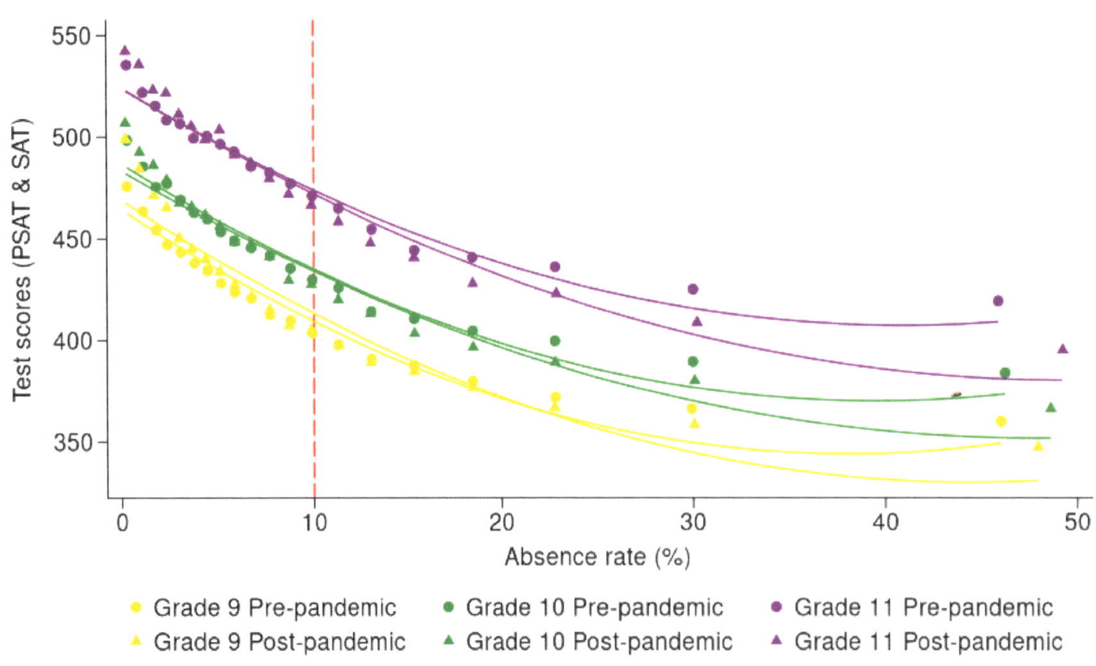

Figure A.2 Students with higher absence rates had lower GPAs in all grades

GPA and absences for middle grade students

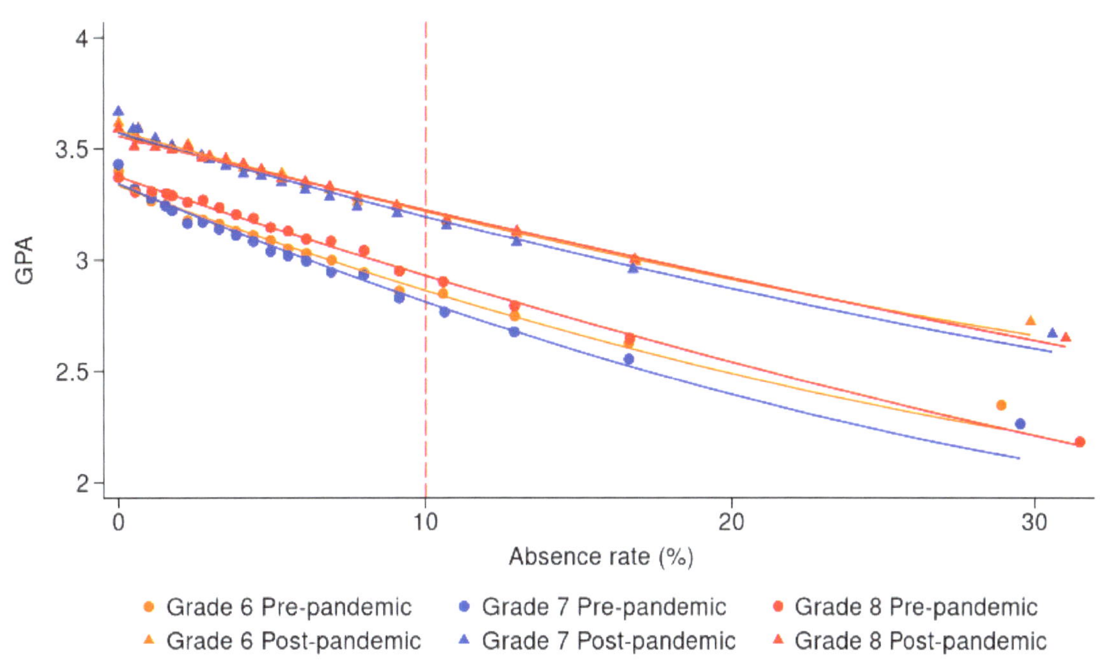

Note: GPA data do not include charter school students.

GPA and absences for high school students

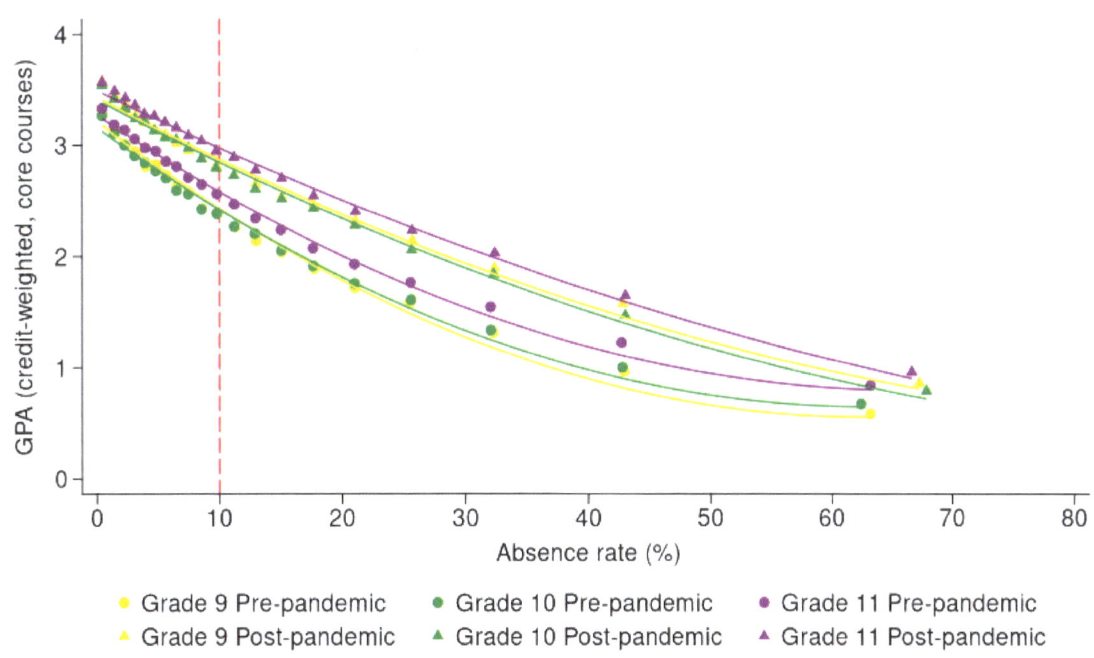

Note: GPA data do not include charter school students.

Relationships of absences with gains on standardized tests

In addition to the figures shown in the report, we also examined the relationship of absences with students' gains on standardized assessments (shown in **Figure A.3**). A student's test gains are computed as the difference between their current score and their score in the prior grade. For eleventh grade, we take the difference between SAT and PSAT because they are vertically aligned. For tenth grade, we take the difference between their PSAT scores. For sixth, seventh, and eighth grade, we take the difference between their PARCC scores (pre-pandemic) or IAR scores (post-pandemic). However, in 2019, when IAR was introduced, we take the difference between IAR and prior grade PARCC, both of which had the same scale.

There were negative relationships between students' absences and their gains from ninth to tenth grade on the PSAT and from tenth to eleventh grade on the PSAT to SAT in both pre- and post-pandemic years. There were also negative relationships for eight-graders in both pre- and post-pandemic years, but these relationships were flatter for sixth- and seventh-graders. While the slopes are similar, the size of the gains were higher in post-pandemic years in the middle grades; students had larger gains in post-pandemic years than students with similar absences in pre-pandemic years.

Figure A.3 Students with higher absence rates had lower test gains in all grades

PARCC and IAR test score gains and absences for middle grade students

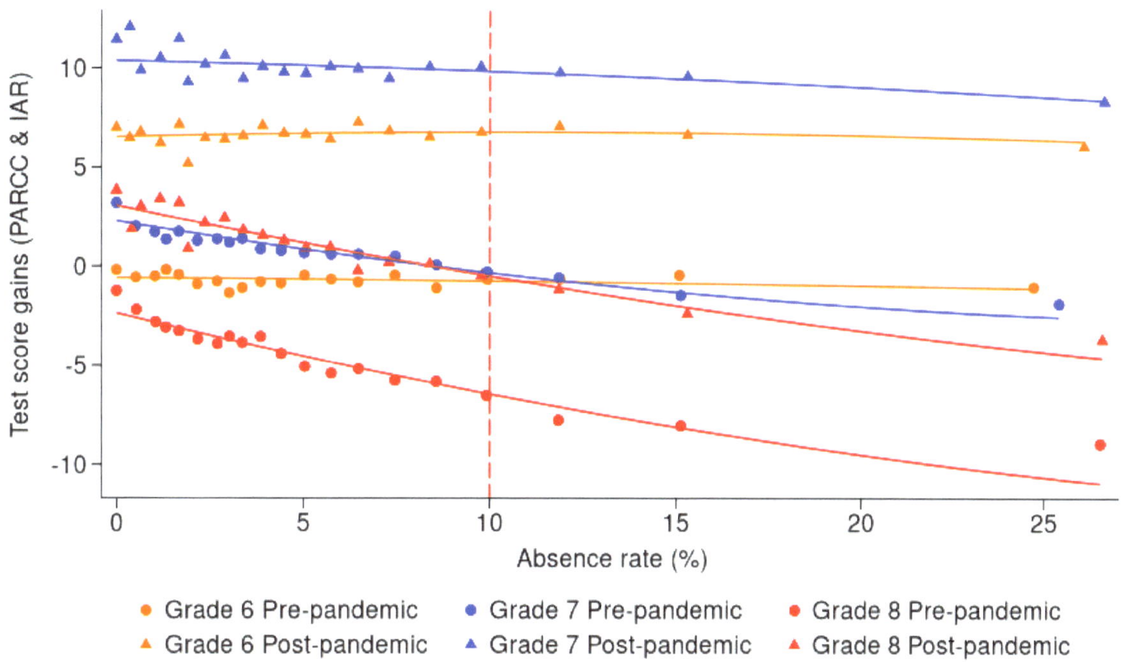

PSAT and SAT test score gains and absences for high school students

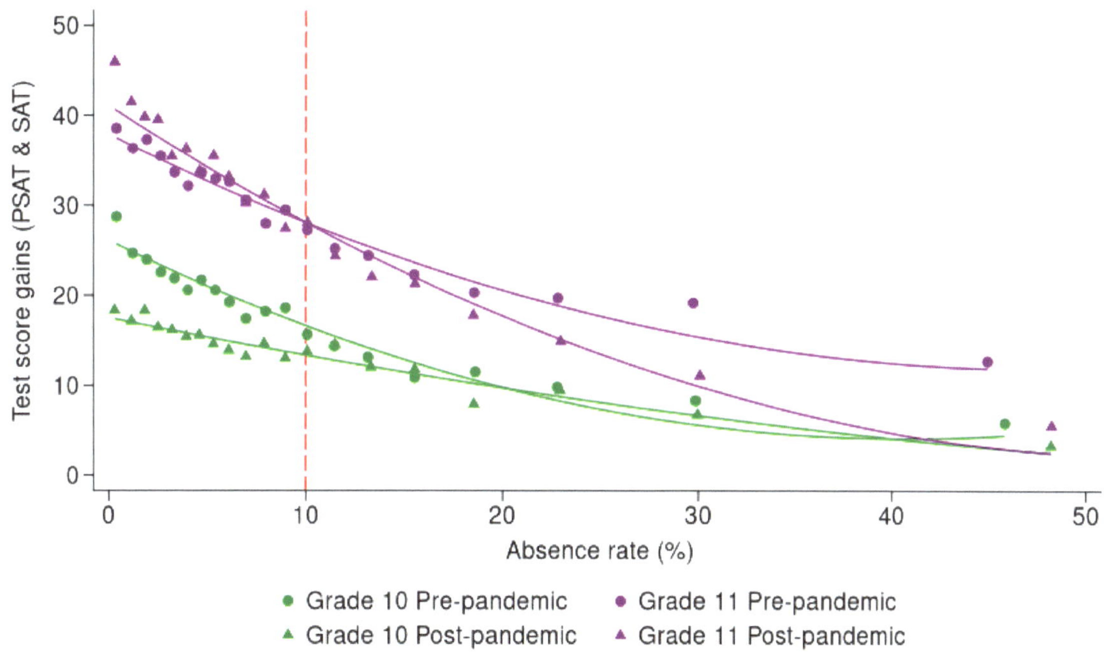

Additional information on Key Finding 3

School absence rates varied considerably, even when comparing schools serving similar students from similar neighborhoods.

The main report displays scatterplots of average absence rates with students grouped by the school they attended (Figure 4) and provides analysis that tracks the school variation after taking into account the variation at the neighborhood where students lived, and then also controls for a series of student characteristics (**Table 1 on p.11**).

We run hierarchical linear models (HLM) that predicted students' absence rates, nesting student observations within their school and then school and the neighborhood where they lived (cross-nested model) to estimate the variation at the school-level and census-tract level. In addition, we control for student characteristics in the cross-nested model to adjust for variation in absence rates between schools that is due to schools serving different student populations. The covariates included are:

- Baseline average absences in grades 3-5 (when predicting absences in the middle grades) or grades 6-8 (when predicting absences in high school)
- Standardized test scores in grades 3-5 (when predicting absences in the middle grades) or grades 6-8 (when predicting absences in high school).
- Demographic characteristics:
  - Race and ethnicity
  - Gender
  - Specific IEP designation
  - Whether they were an English Learner
- Whether they were attending their neighborhood school
- Whether they were in temporary living situations
- Grade level
- Indicators of income and social status in their residential census block group:
  - Percent of families under the poverty line
  - Male unemployment rates
  - Median family income
  - Average education level of adults over age 25

There were 475 schools serving the middle grades and 798 census tracts in which students lived in our analysis before the pandemic and 470 schools and 792 census tracts after the pandemic. In our analysis of grades 9-11 there were 139 schools and 800 census tracts before the pandemic and 131 schools and 793 census tracts after the pandemic.

Table A.4 shows the estimated school standard deviation from the hierarchical models. We used these estimated standard deviations to calculate how different absence rates were for schools and neighborhoods with high absence rates (at the 75th percentile, or 0.6745 standard deviations above the mean) relative to those with low absence rates (at the 25th percentile or 0.6745 standard deviations below the mean), in both pre-pandemic and post-pandemic years, as shown in **Table 1 on p.11**. The estimated school standard deviations show that variation was larger in post-pandemic years than in pre-pandemic years, and larger across high schools than across schools serving grades 6-8. When we took into account the variation that comes from the neighborhood students live in, the variation across schools remained largely the same, declining by 2-6%. When we took into account student characteristics, the variation across schools dropped further by almost one-third, except for schools serving middle grades before the pandemic. There was still substantial variation at the school level even when comparing schools serving similar students.

Table A.4 Estimated school-level standard deviation from hierarchical linear models

		HLM: ***Observations nested in schools*** **No controls**	**Cross-nested HLM:** ***Observations nested in school and neighborhood*** **No controls**	**Cross-nested HLM:** ***Observations nested in school and neighborhood*** **With Covariates**
Grades 6-8	Pre-Pandemic	1.37	1.35	1.13
	Post-Pandemic	2.37	2.23	1.35
Grades 9-11	Pre-Pandemic	5.63	5.42	3.82
	Post-Pandemic	6.85	6.42	4.39

Note: Pre-pandemic years include 2017–19, while post-pandemic years are 2022–24.

Additional information on Key Finding 4

School climate was even more strongly related to school absence after the pandemic than before.

For this part of the analysis, we took the school-level residuals from the cross-nested HLM model with student controls, which are empirical Bayes estimates adjusted for student covariates, and used them to estimate how different school-level measures were related to absence rates among different schools (after we took into account differences in the students they serve, including their students' absence rates in prior years). School-level measures were the average in the three years before the pandemic and the three years after the pandemic. School climate measures came from school average responses on annual surveys of students and teachers in CPS, which had response rates ranging from 71% to 82% among students and 72% to 81% among teachers from 2017 to 2024 (excluding pandemic years). A few schools were not part of these analyses when the measures were not available due to low response rate. For example, instead of 475 middle grade schools in our sample in the pre-pandemic years, we had 470 or 471 schools for these analyses (in the post-pandemic years, 12 middle grade schools lacked two of the measures). For high schools, two or three schools at the most did not have enough answers to calculate a particular measure.

Table A.5 shows the details of the individual school-level measures (*5Essential* school climate) and survey items used for this analysis. Using the school residuals as the dependent variable, we ran regression models with one school-level measure at the time to avoid collinearity among them. The estimated coefficients from these regression equations were transformed to calculate the differences between schools that were in the 25th percentile and the 75th percentile in a measure, based on the fact that a school in the 25th percentile is 0.6745 standard deviation below the mean and one in the 75th percentile is 0.6745 standard deviations above the mean. This is shown in **Figure 6 on p.14**.

Table A.5. Measures of school climate from the 2024–25 *5Essentials* Survey

Measure	Description	Survey Items	Respondent	Reliability
Safety in/around the school	Students feel safe both in and around the school building, and while they travel to and from home.	*How safe do you feel* 1. In the hallways of the school? 2. In the bathrooms of the school? 3. Outside around the school? 4. In your classes?	Student	0.77
Safety from bullying/teasing	Students feels safe from threats, crime or bullying at school.	*How much do you disagree or agree with the following statements?* 1. I worry about crime and violence in this school. 2. Students at this school are often teased or picked on. 3. Students at this school are often threatened or bullied.	Student	0.80
Student peer relationships	Students respect and learn from each other.	*Most students in my school* 1. Like to put others down. 2. Help each other learn. 3. Don't get along together very well. 4. Treat each other with respect.	Student	0.72
School connectedness	Students feel connected and included in the school.	*How much do you disagree or agree with the following statements?* 1. I feel like a real part of my school. 2. People here notice when I'm good at something. 3. Other students in my school take my opinion. 4. People at this school are friendly to me. 5. I'm included in lots of activities at school. 6. I'm excited to go to school everyday.	Student	0.82

Student-Teacher Trust	Students and teachers share a high level of mutual trust and respect.	*How much do you disagree or agree with the following statements?* 1. I feel safe with my teachers at this school 2. I feel comfortable with my teachers at this school. 3. My teachers always keep their promises. 4. My teachers always listen to students' ideas. 5. My teachers treat me with respect.	Student	0.81
Peer Support for Academic Work	Students demonstrate behaviors that lead to academic achievement.	*How many students in your Target class* 1. Feel it is important to attend school everyday? 2. Feel it is important to pay attention in class? 3. Think doing homework is important? 4. Try hard to get good grades?	Student	0.82
Academic Personalism	Teachers connect with students in the classroom and support them in achieving academic goals.	*In my class, my teacher* 1. Notices if I have trouble learning something 2. Explains things in a different way if I don't understand something in class. 3. Gives me specific suggestions about how I can improve my work in this class. 4. Helps catch up if I am behind. 5. Is willing to give extra help on schoolwork if I need it.	Student	0.78
Academic engagement	Students look forward to class, try do their best and find it interesting	*How much do you disagree or agree with the following statements about your Target class?* 1. I usually look forward to this class. 2. I work hard to do my best at this class. 3. Sometimes I get so interested in my work I don't want to stop. 4. The topics we are studying are interesting and challenging.	Student	0.79

Academic Press	Teachers expect students to do their best and to meet academic demands.	*How much do you disagree or agree with the following statements about your Target class?* 1. This class really makes me think. 2. I'm really learning a lot in this class. 3. Expects everyone to work hard. 4. Expects me to do my best all the time. 5. Wants us to become better thinkers, not just memorize things. *In your target class, how often* 1. Are you challenged? 2. Do you have to work hard to do well? 3. Does the teacher ask difficult questions on tests? 4. Does the teacher ask difficult questions in class?	Student	0.75
Teacher-Parent Trust	Teachers and parents are partners in improving student learning.	*1. How many teachers at this school feel good about parents'/guardians' support for their work?* *For the students you teach this year, how many of their parents/guardians.* 2. Support your teaching efforts? 3. Do their best to help their children learn? *4. To what extent do you feel respected by the parents/guardians of your students?* *Please indicate the extent to which you disagree or agree with the following:* 5. Teachers and parents/guardians at this school think of each other as partners in educating children. 6. Staff at this school work hard to build trusting relationships with parents/guardians.	Teacher	0.87

Parent Involvement in School	Parents are active participants in their child's schooling.	*For the students you teach this year, how many of their parents/guardians* 1. Attended parent-teacher conferences when you requested them? 2. Volunteered time to support the school (e.g., volunteer in classrooms, help with school-wide events, etc.)? 3. Contacted you about their child's performance? 4. Responded to your suggestions for helping their child?	Teacher	0.88
Parent Influence on Decision Making in Schools	The school has created opportunities for parents to participate in developing academic programs and influencing school curricula.	*To what extent does this school* 1. Involve parents/guardians in the development of programs aimed at improving students' academic outcomes? 2. Involve parents/guardians in commenting on school curricula? 3. Include parent leaders from all backgrounds in school improvement efforts? 4. Develop formal networks to link all families with each other (e.g., sharing parent directories, providing a website for parents/guardians to connect with one another, etc.)? 5. Encourage more involved parents/guardians to reach out to less involved parents/guardians?	Teacher	0.86

Note: Reliability is derived from a Rasch model using student-level data and ranges from a value of zero (not at all reliable) to 1.0 (perfect reliability).

ABOUT THE AUTHORS*

ELAINE M. ALLENSWORTH is the Lewis-Sebring Director of the UChicago Consortium, where she has conducted research on educational policy and practice for over 25 years. Her research examines factors influencing students' educational attainment, school leadership, and school improvement. She works with policymakers and practitioners to bridge research and practice, serving on panels, policy commissions, and working groups at the local, state and national levels.

MERIL ANTONY is a Senior Research Analyst at the UChicago Consortium. Previously, she served as the Robert Curvin Postdoctoral Associate at the Joseph C. Cornwall Center for Metropolitan Studies, Rutgers University-Newark, where she contributed to freshman on-track projects as part of a research practice partnership with Newark Public Schools. Her research focuses on school organizations, with interests in exploring teacher mindsets, enhancing parent-school relationships, and utilizing use of research evidence to improve student outcomes. Her dissertation, titled Essays on Co-production, Social Equity, and Administration of Schools, delved into the role of socio-cultural mechanisms in shaping school-parent partnerships.

WILLIAM DELGADO is a Senior Research Analyst at the UChicago Consortium. Previously, he was a Research Assistant Professor at Boston University Wheelock College of Education and Human Development. He is an applied micro-economist with research interests in the economics of education, labor economics, and behavioral economics. His overarching goal is to understand and address inequality in opportunities and to foster human potential. William implements a variety of econometric techniques, experimental and quasi-experimental, combined with large-scale administrative data and survey data to answer his research questions. He has researched topics that include teacher quality and parental time investment.

MARISA DE LA TORRE is a Senior Research Associate and Managing Director at the UChicago Consortium. Her research interests include urban school reform, school choice, early indicators of school success, and English Learners. Before joining the UChicago Consortium, Marisa worked for the Chicago Public Schools in the Office of Research, Evaluation, and Accountability. She received a master's degree in economics from Northwestern University.

**Authors are listed in alphabetical order. All authors contributed equally to the study.*

This report reflects the interpretation of the authors. Although the UChicago Consortium's Steering Committee provided technical advice, no formal endorsement by these individuals, organizations, or the full Consortium should be assumed.

UCHICAGO Consortium on School Research

Steering Committee

NATALIE NERIS
Co-Chair
Root and Reimagine Consulting Collective

CARLA RUBALCAVA
Co-Chair
Mikva Challenge

Institutional Members

KIA BANKS
Chicago Principals and Administrators Association

STACY DAVIS GATES
Chicago Teachers Union

SARAH DICKSON
Chicago Public Schools

JASON HELFER
Illinois State Board of Education

MEGAN HOUGARD
Chicago Public Schools

SHANNAE JACKSON
Gwendolyn Brooks College Prep

Individual Members

MARIANA BARRAGAN TORRES
Illinois Workforce and Education Research Collaborative (IWERC)

EURYDICE BEVLY
Carnegie Elementary and Roosevelt University

JESSICA CAÑAS
Kids First Chicago

NANCY CHAVEZ
Gates Foundation

SHARON COLEMAN
Mount Vernon Elementary School

KELLY HALLBERG
University of Chicago Inclusive Economy Lab

MARSHALL HATCH
The Maafa Redemption Project

GREGORY JONES
The Academy Group

BRIAN KELLY
Dr. Martin Luther King Jr. College Prep

AMANDA LEWIS
University of Illinois at Chicago

JORGE MACIAS
Latino Policy Forum

JONATHAN MCKENZIE
Family Center Educational Agency

KAFI MORAGNE-PATTERSON
University of Chicago Inclusive Economy Lab

LILLY PADÍA
Erikson Institute

RITA RAICHOUDHURI
One Million Degrees

TALI RAVIV
Center for Childhood Resilience at Ann & Robert H. Lurie Children's Hospital

ELLEN SCHUMER
Community Organizing and Family Issues (COFI)

ACASIA WILSON FEINBERG
Wilson Feinberg Consultants, LLC

www.ingramcontent.com/pod-product-compliance
Lightning Source LLC
LaVergne TN
LVHW070223110826
845147LV00003B/629

9780984193318